EVERYDAY SHLOKAS, MANTRAS, PRAYERS

AND MORE FOR KIDS

Published by Red Panda, an imprint of Westland Books, a division of Nasadiya Technologies Private Limited, in 2024

No. 269/2B, First Floor, 'Irai Arul', Vimalraj Street, Nethaji Nagar, Alapakkam Main Road, Maduravoyal, Chennai 600095

Westland, the Westland logo, Red Panda and the Red Panda logo are the trademarks of Nasadiya Technologies Private Limited, or its affiliates.

ISBN: 9789360452667
10 9 8 7 6 5 4 3 2 1

Book design by New Media Line Creations, New Delhi

Images sourced from Shutterstock

Printed at Nutech Print Services, India

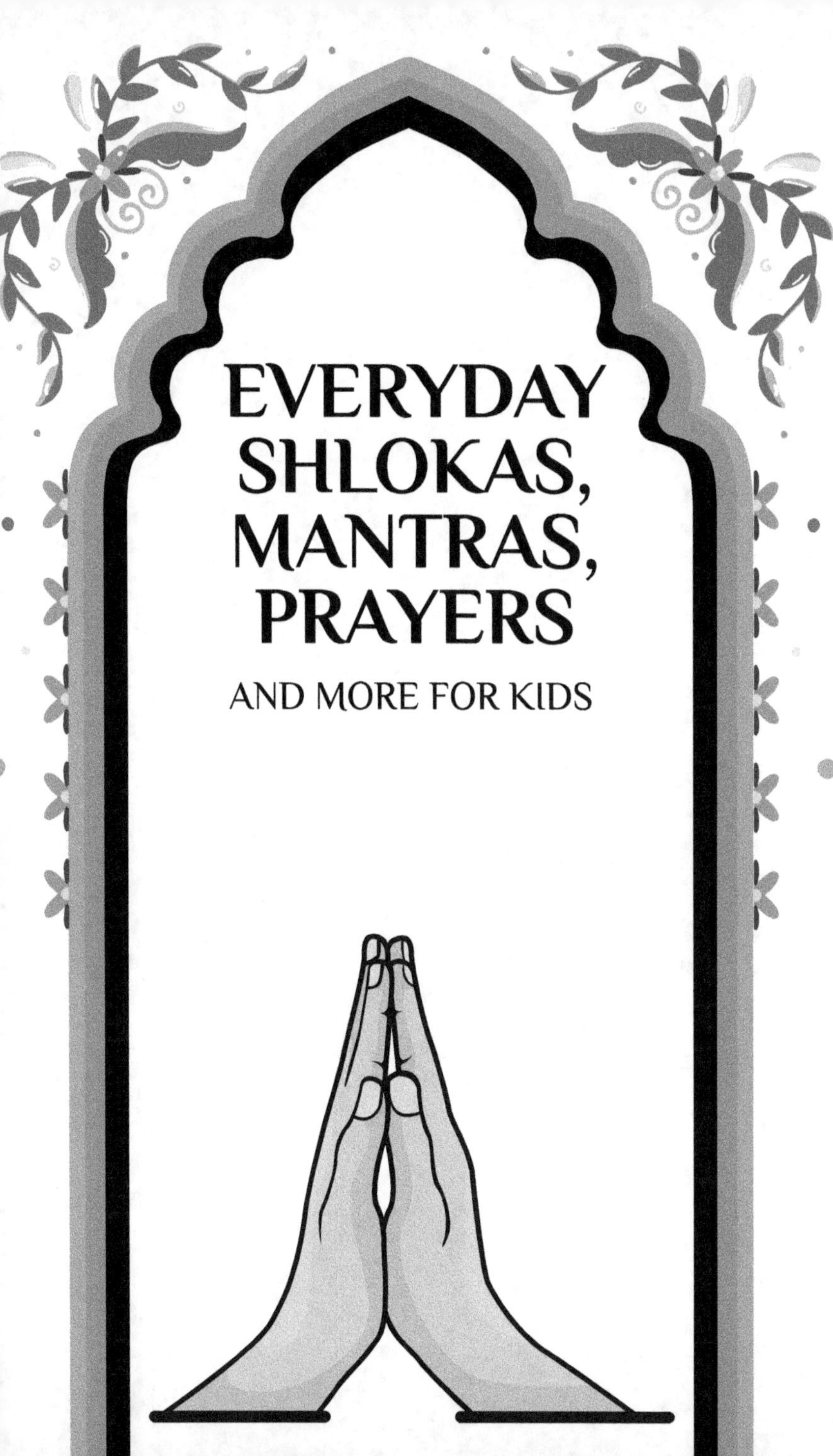
EVERYDAY
SHLOKAS,
MANTRAS,
PRAYERS
AND MORE FOR KIDS

CONTENTS

Introduction

In the hustle and bustle of modern life, it's easy for children to get swept away by the chaos in the world. But what if there was a way to ground them, to infuse their days with moments of peace and gratitude? Enter *Shlokas, Mantras Prayers and More for Kids*, a treasure trove of ancient and contemporary wisdom tailored for young hearts and minds.

Divided into four sections, this book serves as a guiding light through the day, offering shlokas, mantras, stotrams and stutis and prayers for different times of the day—whether waking up with mindfulness, preparing for school with focus or sharing a meal with gratitude. These timeless verses aren't just rituals; they're pathways to positivity, enhancing concentration, pronunciation and communication skills along the way.

But *Shlokas, Mantras Prayers and More for* Kids is more than a recitation manual. It's a journey into the heart of Indian culture, a vibrant tapestry woven with simple yet profound teachings. Each shloka, mantra, stuti, stotram and prayer is a doorway, inviting children to explore the richness of their heritage and deepen their connection to their roots. Moreover, reciting Sanskrit verses improves memory, concentration, and brain function in children. It also aids in healing, stress reduction and cultivates positive thinking, when practiced everyday. Additionally, prayers foster a positive mindset that can transform the entire day.

This book includes Sanskrit verses with their transliteration and its essence to help kids understand the meaning of each verse in simple language. A pronunciation guide, at the end of the book, helps in correct chanting.

With lovely illustrations and easy-to-understand explanations, this book doesn't just teach—it inspires. It creates awareness, imparts knowledge, and fosters a sense of belonging. And as children chant and learn, they're not just repeating words; they're carrying forward a legacy, passing down wisdom from generation to generation.

Shlokas, Mantras, Prayers and More for More isn't just a book—it's a gift. A gift of tradition, of language, of spirituality. It's a reminder that even in the smallest voices, immense power exists to shape the world.

Daily
Shlokas

Starting the Day

गजाननं भूतगणादि सेवितं

कपित्थ जम्बूफलसार भक्षणम् |

उमासुतं शोक विनाशकरणं

नमामि विघ्नेश्वर पादपङ्कजम् ॥

gajānaṇaṃ bhuta-gaṇādi sevitaṃ
kapittha jambū-phalasāra bhakṣaṇam
umā-sutaṃ śoka vināśa-karaṇaṃ
namāmi vighneśvara pāda-paṅkajam

I pay my respect to Lord Ganesha, the deity with an elephant face, who is worshipped by the angels and other heavenly creatures alike. Born to Uma (Parvati), he likes eating the insides of wood apples and rose apples and is the destructor of sorrows. I bow my head and lie down at the feet of Vigneshwara, the God who removes all obstacles.

Upon Waking Up

कराग्रे वसते लक्ष्मीः

करमध्ये सरस्वती ।

करमूले स्थिता गौरी,

मंगलं करदर्शनम् ॥

karāgre vasate lakṣmīḥ
kara-madhye sarasvatī |
kara-mūle sthitā gaurī,
maṅgalaṃ kara-darśanam ||

Goddess Lakshmi lives at the top of our hand, Mother Saraswati in the middle and Mother Gauri (Parvati) at the bottom. Every morning, we look at our hands to feel their divine presence.

Note: It's best to join your palms and gaze at them while you chant this shloka.

Before Stepping Out of the Bed

समुद्रवसने देवि पर्वतस्तनमण्ड ले ।
विष्णुपत्नि नमस्तुभ्यं पादस्पर्शं क्षमस्वमे ॥

samudra-vasane devi parvata-stana-maṇḍale |
viṣṇu-patni namastubhyaṃ pāda-sparśaṃ kṣhamasvame ||

Dear Mother Earth, you wear the ocean like a dress and mountains like your hug. Oh, wife of Lord Vishnu, I bow my head to you. Please forgive me for stepping on your sacred ground.

Note: After saying this prayer, you can gently touch the floor with your hands and seek blessings from Mother Earth.

While Bathing

गङ्गे च यमुने चैव गोदावरि सरस्वति ।
नर्मदे सिन्धु कावेरि जलेऽस्मिन् संनिधिं कुरु ॥

gaṅge cha yamune chaiva godāvari sarasvati
narmade sindhu kāveri jale'smin saṃnidhiṃ kuru

O scared rivers Ganges, Yamuna, Godavari, Sarasvati, Narmada, Sindhu and Kaveri! Please make your presence felt in this water and cleanse my body.

While Lighting a Diya

शुभ कराेत कल्याणमाराेग्य धनसपदा।
शत्रुबुद्धिविनाशाय दीपज्योतिर्नमोऽस्तुते॥

śhubham karoti kalyāṇam-ārogyam dhana-sampadā
śhatru-buddhi-vināśhāya dīpa-jyotir-namostute

I pay my respects to the Lord and the light of the lamp, which brings goodness, health and wealth. Please help me get rid of all negative thoughts in my mind.

Before Going to School

नमस्ते शारदे देवी काश्मीरपुरवासिनि
त्वामहं प्रार्थये नित्यं विद्यादानं च देहि मे ॥

namaste shārade devī kāshmīrapura-vāsini
tvāmahaṃ prārthaye nityaṃ vidyā-dānaṃ cha dehi me ||

Oh, Mother Saraswati, who lives in Kashmir, I pray to you every day. Please help me gain knowledge and succeed in my studies.

Paying Respect to Teachers

गुरू ब्रह्मा गुरू विष्णु,
गुरु देवो महेश्वरा ।
गुरु साक्षात परब्रह्म,
तस्मै श्री गुरुवे नमः ॥

gurū brahmā gurū viṣṇu,
guru devo maheśvarā |
guru sākṣāta para-brahma,
tasmai śrī guruve namaḥ ||

Guru is like Lord Brahma. Guru is like Lord Vishnu. Guru is also like Lord Shiva. Guru represents the Supreme, and I bow down and pay my respects to my gurudev.

Before Studying

सरस्वति नमस्तुभ्यं वरदे कामरूपिणि ।
विद्यारम्भं करिष्यामि सिद्धिर्भवतु मे सदा ॥

sarasvati namastubhyam varade kāma-rūpiṇi
vidyā-rambham kariṣhyāmi siddhir-bhavatu me sadā

I pray to you, Mother Saraswati, goddess of learning who grants all wishes, to bless me. As I start my studies today, please help me succeed now and always.

When in Doubt

ॐ असतो मा सद्गमय ।
तमसो मा ज्योतिर्गमय ।
मृत्योर्मा अमृतं गमय ।
ॐ शान्तिः शान्तिः शान्तिः ॥

oṃ asato mā sad-gamaya |
tamaso mā jyotir-gamaya |
mṛtyormā amṛtaṃ gamaya |
oṃ śāntiḥ śāntiḥ śāntiḥ ||

We ask the Lord to lead us from the unreal to the real, from darkness to light and from death to life forever. Om! May there be peace, peace and more peace!

Overcoming Obstacles

वक्रतुण्ड महाकाय सूर्यकोटि समप्रभ ।
निर्विघ्नं कुरु मे देव सर्वकार्येषु सर्वदा ॥

vakratuṇḍa mahā-kāya sūrya-koṭi samaprabha |
nirvighnaṃ kuru me deva sarva-kāryeṣu sarvadā ||

I pray to you, O respected Lord Ganesha, with your elephant trunk and mighty body shining like countless suns. Please help me overcome any obstacles in my way always and guide me in everything I do.

In Need for Positivity

> आ नो भद्राः क्रतवो यन्तु विश्वतः ।
> ā no bhadrāḥ kratavo yantu viśvataḥ |

I welcome good thoughts coming to me from all directions.

To Calm the Mind

लये संबोधयेत् चित्तं विक्षिप्तं शमयेत् पुनः।
सकषायं विजानीयात् समप्राप्तं न चालयेत् ॥

laye saṃbodhayet cittaṃ vikṣiptaṃ śamayet punaḥ |
sakaśāyaṃ vijānīyāt samaprāptaṃ na cālayet |

Oh, Divine, when my mind feels dull, wake it up. When it gets too excited, calm it down. Along the way, notice any problems that come up. Once my mind feels balanced, let it stay that way.

Before a Meal

अन्नपूर्णे सदापूर्णे शंकर प्राण वल्लभे।
ज्ञान वैराग्य सिध्यर्थं भिक्षां देहि च पार्वति॥

annapūrṇe sadā-pūrṇe śaṃkara prāṇa vallabhe |
jñāna vairāgya sidhyarthaṃ bhikṣāṃ dehi ca pārvati ||

O Mother Annapurna, wife of Lord Shiva and giver of food and happiness! Please grant me wisdom and the ability to let go. Bless me with your love, dear Mother.

For Increasing Will Power

बुद्धिर बलं यशो धैर्य
निर्भयत्वं अरोगतं ।
अजादद्यं वाक् पत्तुत्वं च
हनुमत् स्मरणात् भवेत् ॥

buddhira balaṃ yaśo dhairyaṃ
nirbhaya-tvaṃ arogatam |
ajādadyaṃ vāk pattutvaṃ ca
hanumat smaraṇāt bhavet ||

I ask Lord Hanuman for wisdom, strength, fame, patience, courage and good health. With his help, I'll beat laziness and improve my communication with others.

Before Dinner

ब्रह्मार्पणं ब्रह्म हविर: ब्रह्मग्नौ ब्राह्मण हुतम्;
ब्रह्मैव तेन गन्तव्यम्; ब्रह्म-कर्म-समाधिना

brahm-ārpaṇam brahma havir
brahm-āgnau brahmaṇā hutam
brahmaiva tena gantavyam
brahma-karma-samādhinā

When we're connected to the divine, the food we offer, the spoon we use in the act of offering and even the fire are all sacred. Those who see everything as God find it easy to reach Him.

To Avoid Bad Dreams and the Fear of Darkness

रामं स्कन्दं हनुमंतं वन्तेयं वृकोदरम्।
श्येन यः स्मरेन् नित्यं दुःस्वप्नस् तस्य नश्यति ॥

rāmaṃ skandhaṃ hanumantaṃ vainateyaṃ vṛkodaram |
śayane yaḥ smaren nityam dusvapnas tasya-nashyati ||

I pray to Lord Rama, Skanda, Hanuman, Garuda, and Bheem every night before bed for a peaceful sleep without bad dreams.

Bedtime Prayer

त्वमेव माता च पिता त्वमेव ।
त्वमेव बंधुश्च सखा त्वमेव ।
त्वमेव विद्या द्रविणम् त्वमेव ।
त्वमेव सर्वम् मम देव देव ॥

tvam-eva mātā cha pitā tvam-eva |
tvam-eva bandhuśh-cha sakhā tvam-eva |
tvam-eva vidyā draviṇam tvam-eva |
tvam-eva sarvam mama deva deva ||

You are my mother, father, friend and family too. You are knowledge and you are wealth. Oh my dear Lord, you are everything for me.

Shlokas

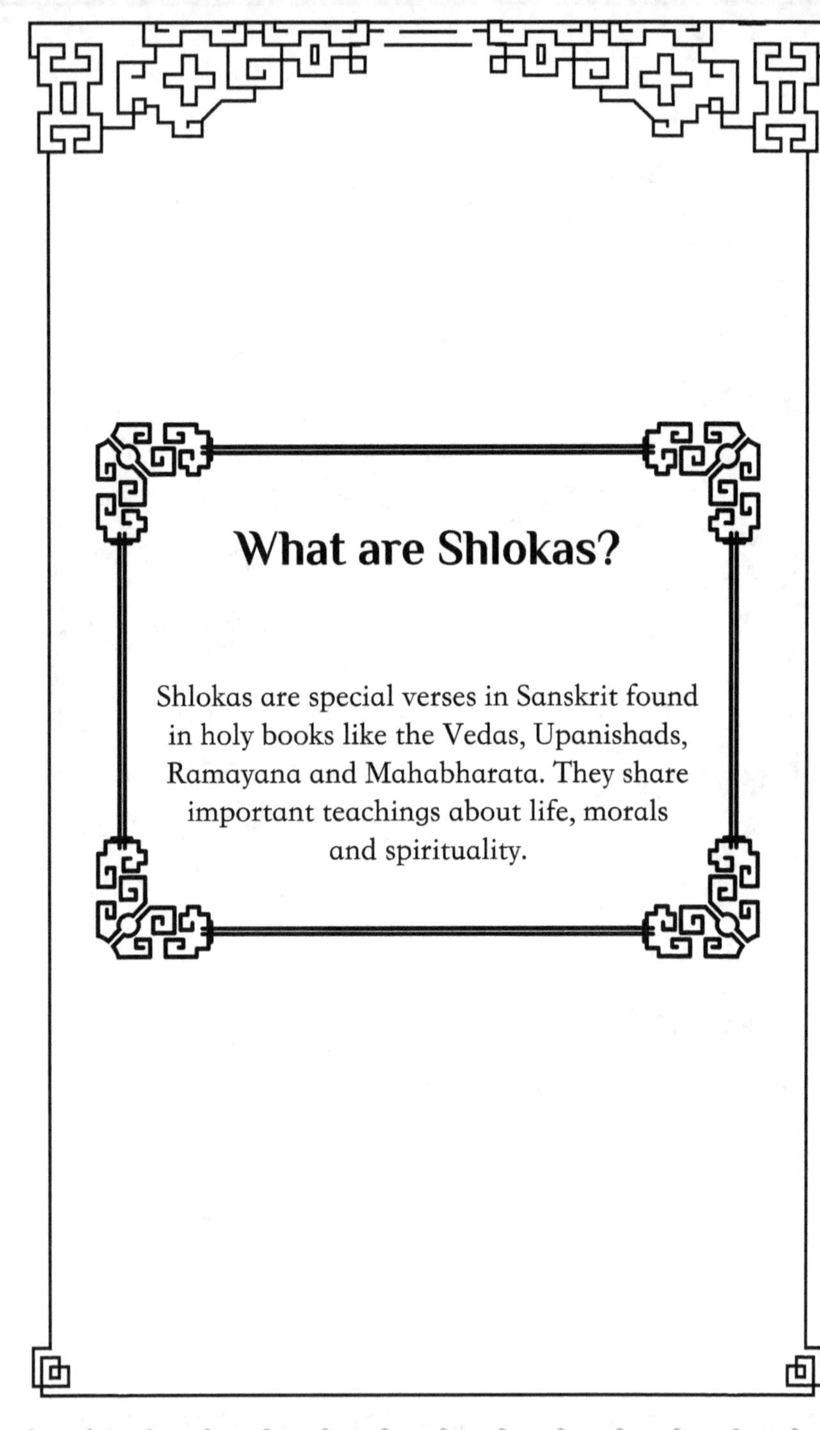

What are Shlokas?

Shlokas are special verses in Sanskrit found in holy books like the Vedas, Upanishads, Ramayana and Mahabharata. They share important teachings about life, morals and spirituality.

Lord Ganesha

मूषिकवाहन मोदकहस्त चामरकर्ण विलम्बितसूत्र ।
वामनरूप महेश्वरपुत्र विघ्नविनायक पाद नमस्ते ॥

mūṣhika-vāhana modaka-hasta
chāmara-karṇa vilambita-sūtra |
vāmana-rūpa maheśhvara-putra
vighna-vināśhaka pāda namaste ||

Seated gracefully on a mouse, holding a sweet modak, with big ears like fans, Lord Ganesh wears a sacred thread that is a symbol of purity and holiness. He's the dear son of Lord Shiva and helps us overcome all obstacles. We respect him and bow to his feet.

Lord Ganesha

अगजानन पद्मार्कं गजाननं अहर्निशम् ।
अनेकदंतं भक्तानां एकदन्तं उपास्महे ॥

agajānana padmārkaṃ gajānanam aharniśam |
anek-adaṃtaṃ bhaktānāṃ ekadantaṃ upāsmahe ||

The loving gaze of Gauri, also known as Devi Parvati, is always on her son Gajanana, who has an elephant face. Similarly, Lord Ganesha blesses his devotees, granting their prayers and wishes. Those who sincerely worship Ekdanta, the one with a single tusk, are forever blessed.

Lord Vishnu

कायेन वाचा मनसेन्द्रियैर्वा
बुद्ध्यात्मना वा प्रकृतेः स्वभावात् ।
करोमि यद्यत्सकलं परस्मै
नारायणयेति समर्पयामि ॥

kāyena vāca manasendriyairvā
buddh-yātmanā vā prakṛteḥ svabhāvāt |
karomi yadyatsakalaṃ parasmai
nārāyaṇayeti samarpayāmi ||

Everything I do—moving, talking, thinking, using my senses and even my feelings deep inside—I offer to Lord Narayana. I dedicate it all to Him. I don't think of it as mine; it's all dedicated to Sri Narayana.

Lord Vishnu

शान्ताकारं भुजगशयनं पद्मनाभं सुरेशं
विश्वाधारं गगनसदृशं मेघवर्णं शुभाङ्गम् ।
लक्ष्मीकान्तं कमलनयनं योगिभिर्ध्यानगम्यं
वन्दे विष्णुं भवभयहरं सर्वलोकैकनाथम् ॥

śāntā-kāraṃ bhujaga-śayanaṃ padmanābhaṃ sureśaṃ
viśvā-dhāraṃ gagan-asadṛśaṃ megha-varṇaṃ śubhāṅgam |
lakṣmī-kāntaṃ kamala-nayanaṃ yogi-bhir-dhyānagamyaṃ
vande viṣṇuṃ bhava-bhaya-haraṃ sarva-loke-ka-nātham ||

I bow to Lord Vishnu, who protects the universe. He peacefully rests on a giant serpent bed, with a lotus growing from his navel, showing his creative power. He supports the whole universe, spreads everywhere like the sky and has a dark, beautiful form. He is the Lord of Mother Lakshmi and is seen by yogis through meditation. I respect Lord Vishnu, who takes away fear and rules over all worlds.

Lord Vishnu

यस्य स्मरण मात्रेण जन्म संसार बन्धनात् ।
विमुच्यते नमस्तस्मै विष्णवे प्रभविष्णवे ॥

yasya smaraṇa-mātreṇa janma sansāra bandhanāt |
vimuchyate namas-tasmai viṣṇave prabha-viṣṇave ||

We bow to Lord Vishnu, the super strong God. Just praying and thinking about him helps break free from being born and dying again and again.

Lord Shiva

कैलासराणा शिव चंद्रमौळी
फणींद्र माथा मुकुटी झळाळी |
कारुण्यसिंधू भवदु:खहारी
तुजवीण शंभो मज कोण तारी ||

kailāsarāṇā śiva chandramaulī
phaṇīṃdra māthā mukuṭī jhalālī |
kāruṇya-siṃdhū bhavadu:khahārī
tuja-vīṇa śaṃbho maja koṇa tārī ||

Oh, Lord Shiva, seated on Mount Kailash, with the moon on your forehead and a serpent as a crown, you're full of kindness and help us see clearly. Who would protect me if it were not for you? I surrender to you for protection, my Lord.

Guru

ध्यानमूलं गुरुर्मूर्तिः
पूजामूलं गुरुर्पदम् ।
मन्त्रमूलं गुरुर्वाक्यं
मोक्षमूलं गुरूकृपा ॥

dhyana-mūlaṃ gurur-mūrtiḥ
pūjā-mūlaṃ gurur-padam |
mantra-mūlaṃ gurur-vākyaṃ
mokṣa-mūlaṃ gurūr-kṛpā ||

Meditation starts with the Guru's form. Worship begins at the Guru's feet. Mantras come from the Guru's words. And liberation comes from the Guru's grace.

Brahma Vishnu Mahesh (Trimurti)

ब्रह्मा मुरारि स्त्रिपुरान्तकारी
भानुः शशी भूमिसुतो बुधश्च ।
गुरुश्च शुक्रः शनिराहुकेतवः
कुर्वन्तु सर्वे मम सुप्रभातम् ॥

brahmā murāri stripurāntakārī
bhānuḥ śaśī bhūmi-suto budhaśca |
guruśca śukraḥ śani-rāhu-ketavaḥ
kurvantu sarve mama suprabhātam||

The gods Brahma, Murari (Krishna or Vishnu) and Shiva, the one who defeated the Tripurasuras, along with the planets Sun, Moon, Mars, Mercury, Jupiter, Venus, Saturn and the lunar nodes Rahu and Ketu, make my mornings lucky.

Lord Krishna

कृष्णाय वासुदेवाय देवकी नन्दनाय च ।
नन्दगोप कुमाराय गोविन्दाय नमो नमः ॥

kṛṣṇāya vāsudevāya devakī nandanāya ca |
nanda-gopa kumārāya govindāya namo namaḥ |

We bow to Lord Krishna, the son and joy of Vasudeva and Devaki, Nand's boy and the Lord Govinda. We bow to Him again and again.

Lord Ram

रामाय रामभद्राय रामचन्द्राय वेधसे।
रघुनाथाय नाथाय सीतायाः पतये नमः॥२॥

rāmāya rāma-bhadrāya rāmachandrāya vedhase |
raghunāthāya nāthāya sītāyāḥ pataye namaḥ ||

We greet the great Lord Ram, also known as Ramabhadra and Ramachandra. He's known as Raghunath, the Supreme Master and Sita's husband.

Lord Hanuman

अतुलितबलधामं हेमशैलाभदेहं
दनुजवनकृशानुं ज्ञानिनामग्रगण्यम् ।
सकलगुणनिधानं वानराणामधीशं
रघुपतिप्रियभक्तं वातात्मजं नमामि ॥

atulit-abaladhāmaṃ hema-śailābha-dehaṃ
danuja-vana-kṛśānuṃ jñāninām-agragaṇyam |
sakala-guṇani-dhānaṃ vānarā-ṇamadhīśaṃ
raghupati-priya-bhaktaṃ vātātmajaṃ namāmi||

Hanuman, the son of the wind god, is home to supreme strength. His body gleams like the golden mountain (Sumeru). He's brave against demons, wise, full of good qualities and the leader of all monkeys. I bow to him, the one who is dear to Lord Ram.

Lord Hanuman

मनोजवम मारुत तुल्य वेगम,
जितेंद्रियम बुद्धिमतां वरिष्ठं ।
वातात्मजं वानारायूथ मुख्यम,
श्रीराम दूतं शरणम प्रपद्ये ॥

manoja-vama māruta tulya vegama,
jitendriyama buddhi-matāṃ variṣṭhaṃ |
vātāt-majaṃ vānārā-yūtha mukhyama,
śrī-rāma dūtaṃ śaraṇama prapadye ||

I seek shelter in Lord Hanuman. I pray to the one who is faster than thought, stronger than the wind, wiser than the wisest and the son of the Wind God. He leads the monkey army and is Lord Ram's messenger. I bow to you, O Hanuman!

Lord Hanuman

अंजना नंदनं वीरं, जानकी शोक नाशनं ।
कपीश मक्ष हंतारं, वंदे लंका भयंकरं ॥

añjanā-nandanam vīram
jānakī-śhoka-nāśhanam |
kapīśham akṣha hantāram
vande laṅkā bhayaṅ-karam ||

We respectfully bow to Lord Hanuman, brave son of Anjana and the king of monkeys. He brought joy back to Mother Sita and defeated Ravan's son, making Lanka shiver in fear.

Mother Earth

नमो देव्यै महादेव्यै शिवायै सततं नमः।
नमः प्रकृत्यै भद्रायै नियताः प्रणताः स्म ताम्॥

namo devyai mahā-devyai śivāyai satataṃ namaḥ |
namaḥ prakṛtyai bhadrāyai niyatāḥ praṇatāḥ sma tām ||

We bow to the Goddess, to the great source of goodness. We lay flat on the floor, bowing to Nature with folded hands.

Goddess Parvati

सर्वमङ्गलमाङ्गल्ये शिवे सर्वार्थसाधिके ।
शरण्ये त्र्यम्बके गौरि नारायणि नमोऽस्तु ते ॥

sarva-maṅgala-māṅgalye śive sarvārtha-sādhike |
śaraṇye tryambake gauri nārāyaṇi namo'stu te||

We bow to Mother Parvati, who is very kind and brings happiness to the world. She's Shiva's wife, Vishnu's sister and protects all living creatures—demons, humans and gods.

Lord Krishna

करारविन्देन पदारविन्दं
मुखारविन्दे विनिवेशयन्तम्।
वटस्य पत्रस्य पुटे शयानं
बालं मुकुन्दं मनसा स्मरामि।।

karāra-vindena pādā-ravindaṃ
mukhā-ravinde vinave śayantam

I focus on baby Krishna, sleeping on a banyan leaf, with his lotus like foot in his lotus like mouth, with his hand like a lotus flower.

Goddess Saraswati

या कुन्देन्दुतुषारहारधवला
या शुभ्रवस्त्रावृता
या वीणावरदण्डमण्डितकरा
या श्वेतपद्मासना।
या ब्रह्माच्युत
शंकरप्रभृतिभिर्देवैः सदा वन्दिता
सा मां पातु सरस्वती
भगवती निःशेषजाड्यापहा ॥१॥

yā kundendu-tushāra-hāra-dhavalā
yā shubhra-vastrāvṛitā
yā vīṇā-vara-daṇḍa-maṇḍita-karā
yā śhveta-padmāsanā
yā brahmāchyuta
śhankara-prabhṛtibhir devaiḥ sadā vanditā
sā mām pātu sarasvatī
bhagavatī niḥśheṣa-jādyāpahā

We bow to Mother Saraswati, who's as fair as jasmine flowers. She wears white clothes and a necklace as white as snow. She holds a veena and a special staff. She sits on a pure white lotus and is worshipped by Brahma, Vishnu, Shiva and all the gods. We ask her to help us understand and keep us safe.

Goddess Lakshmi

नमस्तेऽस्तु महामाये
श्रीपीठे सुरपूजिते ।
शङ्खचक्रगदाहस्ते
महालक्ष्मि नमोऽस्तुते ॥

namaste'stu mahā-māye
śrīpīṭhe sura-pūjite |
śaṅkha-cakra-gadā-haste
mahā-lakṣmi namo'stute||

I pay my respects to Goddess Lakshmi, who helps create everything and is worshipped by the gods. Salute to the Goddess who carries a conch, disc and mace. I bow to you with respect.

Goddess Durga

<blockquote>
या देवी सर्वभूतेषु शक्ति-रूपेण संस्थिता।
नमस्तस्यै नमस्तस्यै नमस्तस्यै नमो नमः॥

yā devī sarva-bhūteṣu śakti-rūpeṇa saṃsthitā |
namastasyai namastasyai namastasyai namo namaḥ ||
</blockquote>

O Goddess Durga, you are everywhere. Even when we sleep. I bow to you humbly. I salute you three times. You are the sleep that's in all living things.

Knowledge

विद्यां ददाति विनयं
विनयाद् याति पात्रताम् |
पात्रत्वात् धनमाप्नोति
धनात् धर्मं ततः सुखम् ||

vidyāṃ dadāti vinayaṃ
vinayād yāti pātratām |
pātratvāt dhana-māpnoti
dhanāt dharmaṃ tataḥ sukham ||

Knowledge gives you discipline. Discipline comes from being good. Being good helps you get wealth. With wealth, you can do good things. When you have all these, you feel happy and joyful.

Mantras

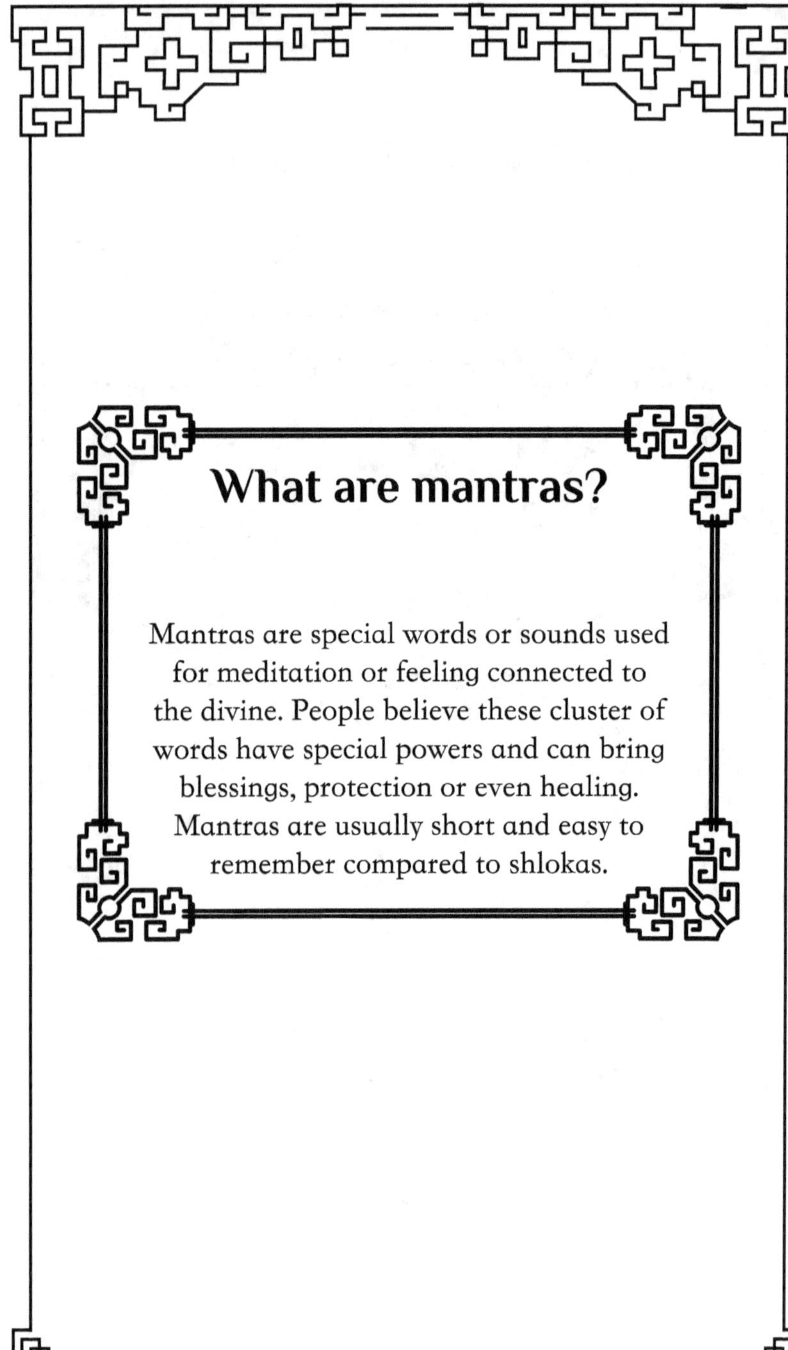

What are mantras?

Mantras are special words or sounds used for meditation or feeling connected to the divine. People believe these cluster of words have special powers and can bring blessings, protection or even healing. Mantras are usually short and easy to remember compared to shlokas.

Ganesh Mantra

एकदन्ताय विद्महे वक्रतुण्डाय धीमहि ।
तन्नो दन्ती प्रचोदयात् ॥

ekadantāya vidmahe
vakratuṇḍāya dhīmahi
tanno dantiḥ prachodayāt

I pray to Lord Ganesh, with his big elephant head and one tusk, to give me knowledge and help me understand things better. I pray to the one with a curved trunk, may my mind always think about him.

Ganesh Mantra

गणानां त्वा गणपतिं हवामहे
कविं कवीनामुपमश्रवस्तमम् ।
ज्येष्ठराजं ब्रह्मणां ब्रह्मणस्पत
आ नः शृण्वन्नूतिभिः सीद सादनम् ॥

ganānāṃ tvā gaṇapatiṃ havāmahe
kaviṃ kavīnām-upamaśravastamam |
jyeṣṭha-rājaṃ brahmaṇāṃ brahmaṇaspata
ā naḥ śṛṇvannūtibhiḥ sīda sādanam ||

I pray to you, O Ganapati, the leader of all of Lord Shiva's helpers, also known as the ganas. You are wise and respected, like a king of prayers. Please listen to my prayers and help me make them strong and smart. O Ganapati, chief of all, you are wise and famous. Please bless my offerings and fill them with your power and wisdom.

Ganesha Mantra

ॐ ग गणपतयं नमो नम:
श्री सिध्धीविनायक नमो नम: ।
अष्टविनायक नमो नम:
गणपती बाप्पा मोरया ॥

oṁ gan gaṇapataye namo namaḥ
śhrī siddhi-vināyaka namo namaḥ |
aṣhṭa-vināyaka namo namaḥ
gaṇapatī bāppā morayā ||

I sing songs about the greatness of Lord Ganesh, who gives His powers to His followers. He appears in eight different forms. I honour Lord Ganapati, the leader of Lord Shiva's special allies, the ganas, who is like an elder brother to me.

Gayatri Mantra

ॐ भूर्भुवः स्वः तत्सवितुर्वरेण्यं।
भर्गो देवस्य धीमहि धियो यो नः प्रचोदयात् ॥

oṃ bhūrbhuvaḥ svaḥ tat-savi-tur-vareṇyam |
bhargo devasya dhīmahi dhiyo yo naḥ pracodayāt ||

Om! I focus on the divine light of the sun, the source of all life. Its light shines everywhere—in my world, in my thoughts and in my spirits. May it guide my mind and give me wisdom. May it help me think clearly and live rightly.

Maha Mrityunjay Mantra

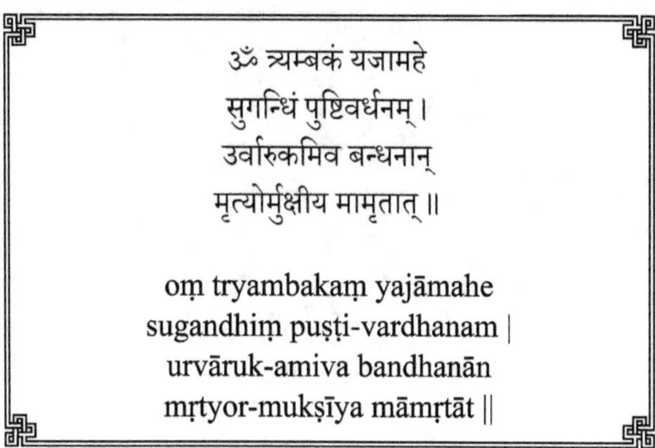

We pray to the three-eyed Lord Shiva. He makes life sweet and full of good things. He can free us from the cycle of life and death as easily as a pumpkin falls off its vine. We pray to Him to free us from this cycle of life and grant us immortality.

Shiva Mantra

ॐ त्र्यम्बकं यजामहे
सुगन्धिं पुष्टिवर्धनम् ।
उर्वारुकमिव बन्धनान्
मृत्योर्मुक्षीय मामृतात् ॥

karpūra-gauraṃ karuṇā-vatāraṃ
saṃsāra-sāram bhujagendra-hāram |
sadā-vasantaṃ hṛdayā-ravinde
bhavaṃ bhavānī-sahitaṃ namāmi ||

Lord Shiva, who is as white and pure as camphor, is full of love and kindness. The whole universe is within Him. He wears a snake (Vasuki) around His neck. We pray to the Lord, who lives in my heart with Mother Parvati (Bhavani), forever.

Shiva Mantra

करचरणकृतं वाक् कायजं कर्मजं वा
श्रवणनयनजं वा मानसंवापराधं ।
विहितं विहितं वा सर्व मेतत् क्षमस्व
जय जय करुणाब्धे श्री महादेव शम्भो ॥

kara-charaṇa-kṛtaṃ vāk kāyajaṃ karmajaṃ vā
śravaṇa-nayanajaṃ vā mānasaṃ-vāparādham |
vihitaṃ vihitaṃ vā sarva metat kṣamasva
jaya jaya karuṇā-bdhe śrī mahādeva śambho ||

Dear Lord Shiva, please forgive all my wrong doing, using my hands, feet or speech, or with my senses (like seeing or hearing), or even with my thoughts. I worship you, my kind Lord Shiva. You're super awesome and forgiving, so please keep being kind to me.

Shanti Mantra

ॐ सह नाववतु ।
सह नौ भुनक्तु ।
सह वीर्यं करवावहै ।
तेजस्वि नावधीतमस्तु मा विद्विषावहै ।
ॐ शान्तिः शान्तिः शान्तिः ॥

oṃ saha nāvavatu |
saha nau bhunaktu |
saha vīryaṃ karavāvahai |
tejasvi nāvadhītamastu mā vidviṣāvahai |
oṃ śāntiḥ śāntiḥ śāntiḥ ||

May the big protector keep both student and teacher safe and help us grow together.

May we, student and teacher, work together with energy and make our learning great. Let's not fight. Let there be light and peace for everyone.

Shanti Mantra

ॐ पूर्णमदः पूर्णमिदं पूर्णात्पूर्णमुदच्यते ।
पूर्णस्य पूर्णमादाय पूर्णमेवावशिष्यते ॥
ॐ शान्तिः शान्तिः शान्तिः ॥

oṃ pūrṇam-adaḥ pūrṇam-idaṃ pūrṇāt-pūrṇa-mudacyate |
pūrṇasya pūrṇa-mādāya pūrṇa-mevāvaśiṣyate ||
oṃ śāntiḥ śāntiḥ śāntiḥ ||

God is the highest truth. The ultimate reality. It's above everything. Even when you take it away from everything, it's still there. May peace be there, always!

Shanti Mantra

ॐ सह नाववतु ।
सह नौ भुनक्तु ।
सह वीर्यं करवावहै ।
तेजस्वि नावधीतमस्तु मा विद्विषावहै ।
ॐ शान्तिः शान्तिः शान्तिः ॥

oṁ sarveṣhām svastir-bhavatu |
sarveṣhām śhantir-bhavatu |
sarveṣhām pūrṇam bhavatu |
sarveṣhām maṅgalam bhavatu |
oṁ śhāntiḥ śhāntiḥ śhāntiḥ ||

We pray to the Supreme Lord for the good health of all beings. We call on Him for peace, fulfilment and prosperity for all living beings. May peace prevail.

Shanti Mantra

ॐ सर्वेषां स्वस्तिर्भवतु ।
सर्वेषां शान्तिर्भवतु ।
सर्वेषां पूर्णंभवतु ।
सर्वेषां मंगलंभवतु ।
ॐ शांतिः शांतिः शांतिः ॥

om̐ sarve bhavantu sukhinaḥ
sarve santu nirāmayāḥ |
sarve bhadrāṇi paśhyantu
mā kaśhchid duḥkha-bhāgbhavet ||
om̐ śhāntiḥ śhāntiḥ śhāntiḥ ||

We pray to God for good health for all living beings. We ask Him for peace, happiness and prosperity. May there be no suffering and may peace be everywhere.

Mangal Mantra

लोका: समस्ता: सुखिनो भवन्तु

Lokah Samastah Sukhino Bhavantu

May all beings on this earth be happy and free. May our thoughts, words and actions help make this happiness and freedom possible for all.

Guru Mantra

ॐ अज्ञानतिमिरान्धस्य ज्ञानाञ्जनशालाकया
चक्षुरुन्मीलितं येन तस्मै श्रीगुरवे नमः

oṁ ajñāna-timirāndhasya jñānāñjana-śhalākayā
chakṣur unmīlitam yena tasmai śhrī-gurave namaḥ

Om! We respectfully bow to the Spiritual Master who removes our ignorance with the light of divine knowledge. He opens our eyes and helps us see the truth. He opens our eyes, enabling us to see the truth.

Ram Mantra

शुद्धब्रह्मपरात्पर राम् ।
कालात्मकपरमेश्वर राम् ॥
शेषतल्पसुखनिद्रित राम् ।
ब्रह्माद्यामरप्रार्थित राम् ॥
राम् राम् जय राजा राम् ।
राम् राम् जय सीता राम् ॥

śhuddha-brahma-parātpara-rāma |
kālātmaka-parameśhvara-rāma ||
śheṣha-talpa-sukha-nidrita-rāma |
brahmādhyamara-prārthita-rāma ||
rāma rāma jaya rājā rāma |
rāma rāma jaya sītā rāma ||

We sing the glories of Lord Ram, who is the Supreme Almighty. He is the controller of time and destiny. He rests blissfully in yoga-nidra on the divine serpent, Ananta Shesh (as Lord Vishnu). All the gods and goddesses, including Brahma, offer their prayers to Him. May Lord Ram be victorious! May Sita and Ram be triumphant!

Vedic Shanti Mantra

ॐ भद्रं कर्णेभिः शृणुयाम देवाः ।
भद्रं पश्येमाक्षभिर्यजत्राः ।
स्थिरैरङ्गैस्तुष्टुवाँसस्तनूभिः ।
व्यशेम देवहितं यदायुः ।

om̐ bhadram karṇebhiḥ śhriṇuyāma devāḥ
bhadram paśhyemākṣhabhiryajatrāḥ
sthirairaṅgaistuṣhṭtuvāñgsastanūbhiḥ
vyaśhema devahitam yadāyuḥ
svasti na indro vṛiddhaśhravāḥ
svasti naḥ pūṣhā viśhvavedāḥ
svasti nastārkṣhyo ariṣhṭanemiḥ
svasti no bṛihaspatirdadhātu
om̐ śhāntiḥ śhāntiḥ śhāntiḥ

We pray to the Lord to help us hear good things and see good things. With steady senses and our bodies in prayer, may we live a long and fulfilling life. May Indra bless us with well-being.

Sai Mantra

ॐ साईं नमो नमः

श्री साईं नमो नमः,
जय जय साईं नमो नमः
सतगुरु साईं नमो नमः

oṃ sāi namo namaḥ
śrī sāi namo namaḥ
jaya jaya sāi namo namaḥ
sataguru sāi namo namaḥ

We bow down to Sai Baba and pray to Him. He is the real Guru. We pay our respects to Him.

Om Mani Padme Mantra

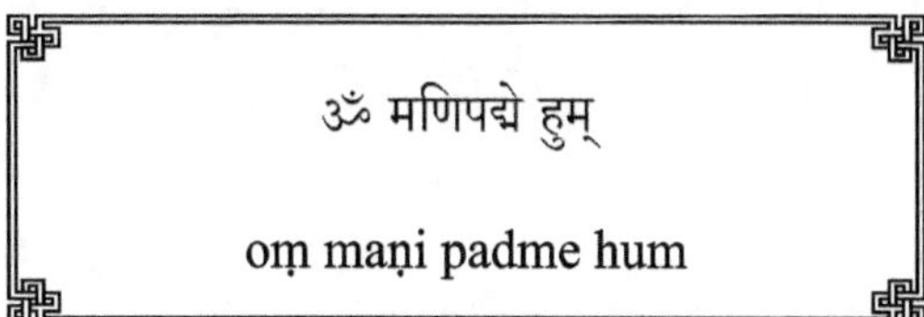

According to the Fourteenth Dalai Lama, 'Om Mani Padme Hum' means that by being kind and wise in life, we can become like a Buddha in our body, words, and thoughts.

Stotrams
and Stutis

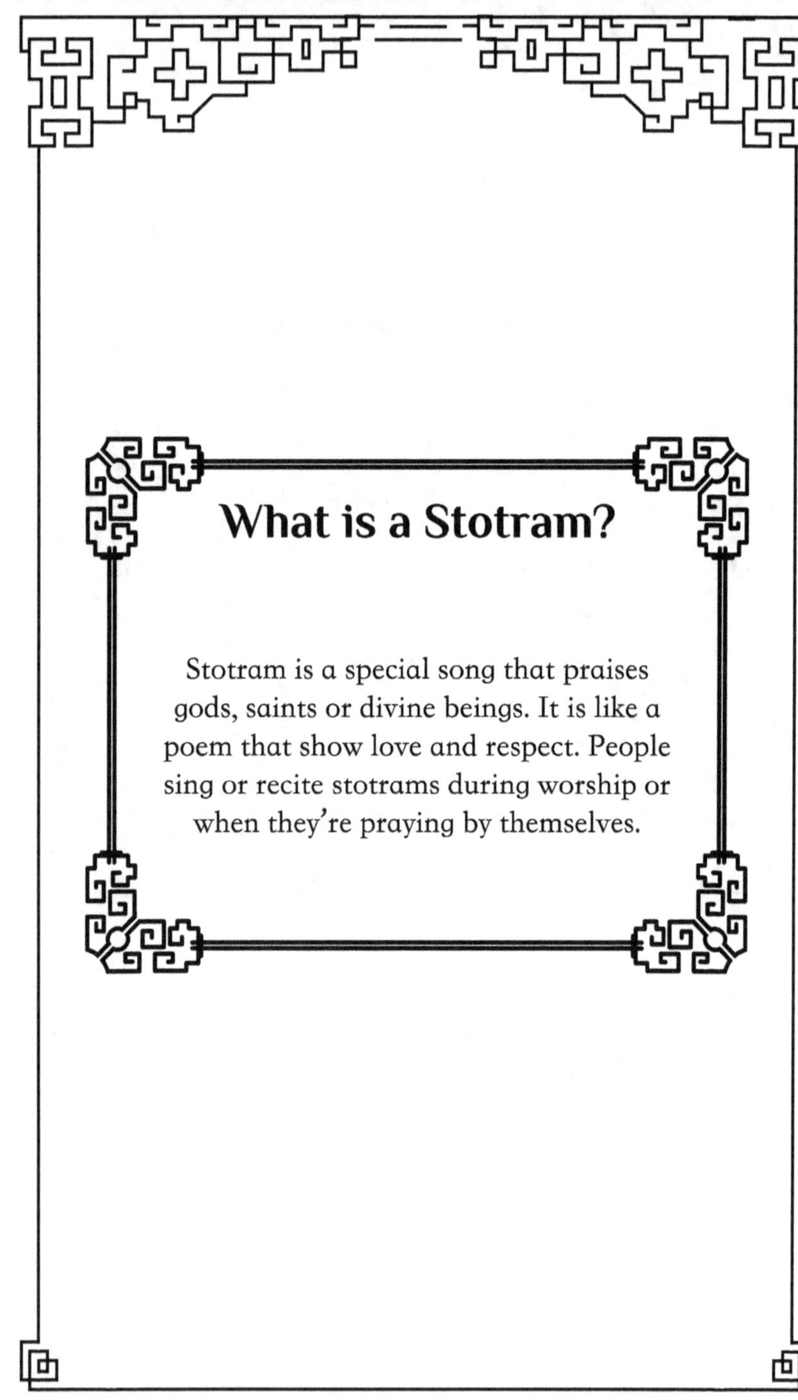

What is a Stotram?

Stotram is a special song that praises gods, saints or divine beings. It is like a poem that show love and respect. People sing or recite stotrams during worship or when they're praying by themselves.

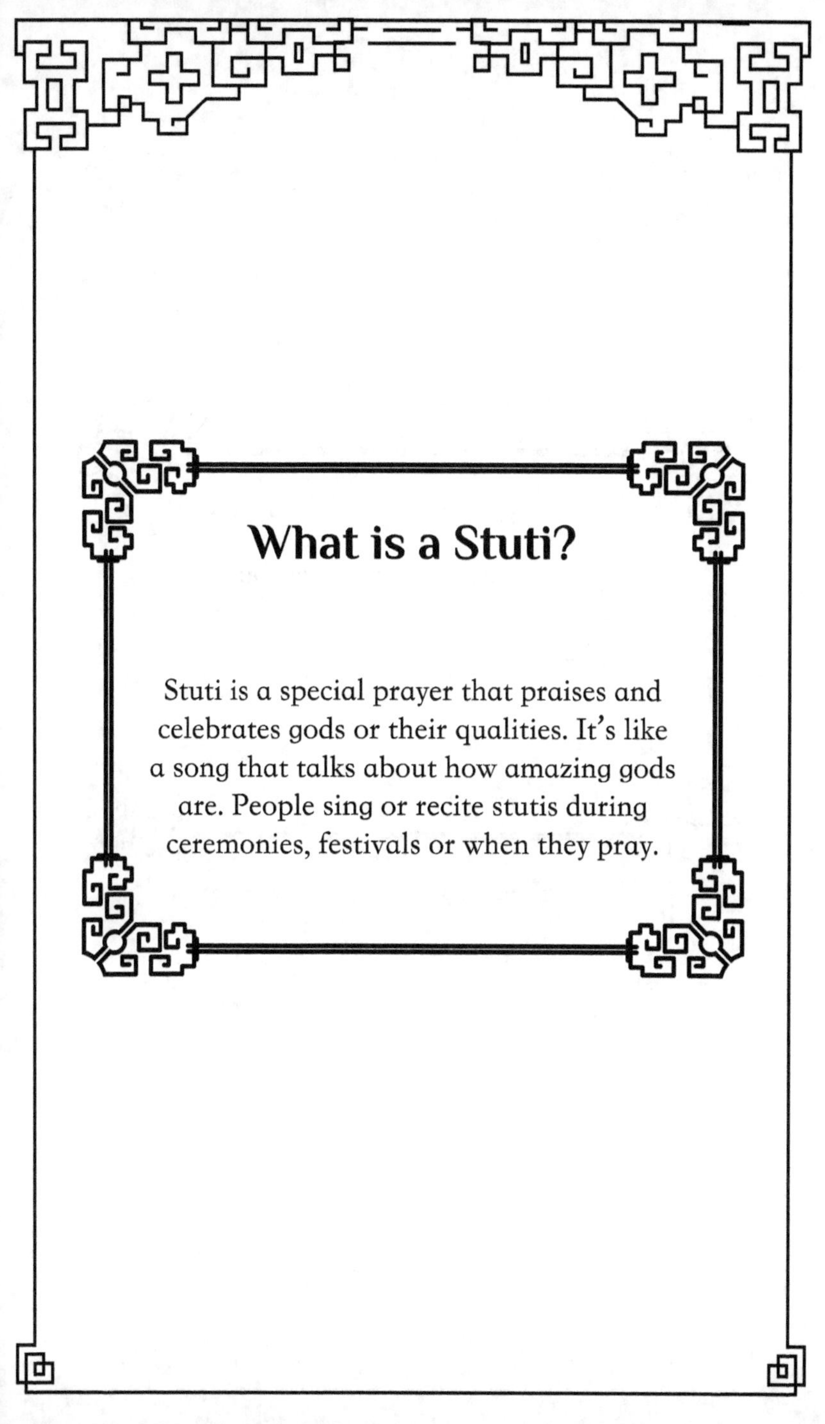

What is a Stuti?

Stuti is a special prayer that praises and celebrates gods or their qualities. It's like a song that talks about how amazing gods are. People sing or recite stutis during ceremonies, festivals or when they pray.

Most stotrams are long songs, but here are some shorter versions to keep it simple. These abbreviated stotrams are easy to remember, chant or sing.

Sankat Nashan Ganesh Stotram

प्रणम्य शिरसा देवं गौरीपुत्र विनायकम् ।
भक्तावासं स्मरेन्नित्यायुष्कामार्थसिद्धये ॥

praṇamya śirasā devaṃ gaurīputra vināyakam |
bhaktāvāsaṃ smaren-nity-āyuṣ-kāmārtha-siddhaye ||

I bow to Lord Ganesha, the son of Gauri and the remover of all obstacles. I pray to him with devotion, asking for his many blessings. May this mantra give me a long life where my wishes come true.

Ganesh Stotram for Wish-fulfillment

विद्यार्थी लभते विद्यां
धनार्थी लभते धनम्।
पुत्रार्थी लभते पुत्रान्
मोक्षार्थी लभते गतिम् ॥

vidyārthī labhate vidya
dhanārthī labhate dhanam |
putrārthī labhate putrān
mokṣārthī labhate gatim ||

If you want knowledge, may you get it; if you want money, may you get it; if you want a child, may you get it; if you want salvation, may you reach it.

Shiv Stotram

जटाटवीगलज्जलप्रवाहपावितस्थले
गलेऽवलम्ब्य लम्बितां भुजङ्गतुङ्गमालिकाम् ।
डमड्डमड्डमड्डमन्निनादवड्डमर्वयं
चकार चण्डताण्डवं तनोतु नः शिवः शिवम् ॥१॥

jaṭāṭavīgalajjalapravāhapāvitasthale
gale'valambya lambitāṃ bhujaṅgatuṅgamālikām |
ḍamaḍḍamaḍḍamaḍḍamanninādavaḍḍamarvayaṃ
cakāra caṇḍatāṇḍavaṃ tanotu naḥ śivaḥ śivam ||

From the forest of his matted hair, water flows and wets his neck, where a giant snake hangs like a garland. His drum plays damat, damat, damat, damat, and Shiva dances with great energy to bless us and bring prosperity.

... this stotram is continued to the next page

Shiv Stotram

जटाकटाहसम्भ्रमभ्रमन्निलिम्पनिर्झरी_
विलोलवीचिवल्लरीविराजमानमूर्धनि ।
धगद्धगद्धगज्जलल्ललाटपट्टपावके
किशोरचन्द्रशेखरे रतिः प्रतिक्षणं मम ॥

jaṭākaṭāhasambhramabhramannilimpanirjharī_
vilolavīcivallarīvirājamānamūrdhani
dhagaddhagaddhagajjalallalāṭapaṭṭapāvake
kiśoracandraśekhare ratiḥ pratikṣaṇaṃ mama

The river flows through his matted hair, making his head shine with gentle waves. His forehead glows like a brilliant fire, and a crescent moon decorates his head. This makes me love him more and more every second.

Krishna Stuti

अच्युतं केशवं रामनारायणं
कृष्णदामोदरं वासुदेवं हरिम् ।
श्रीधरं माधवं गोपिकावल्लभं
जानकीनायकं रामचंद्रं भजे ॥

achyutam keśhavam rāma-nārāyaṇam
kṛishṇa-dāmodaram vāsudevam harim |
śhrīdharam mādhavam gopikā-vallabham
jānakī-nāyakam rāmachandram bhaje ||

We sing the praises of Lord Krishna who is so attractive and has many names, like Vasudev, Damodar, Hari, Sridhar, Madhav, Ram and Narayan. He never makes mistakes and is the slayer of the demon Keshi. As Lord Krishna, he is loved by the gopis. As Lord Ram, he is loved by Mother Sita.

Krishna Stotram

वसुदेवसुतं देवं कंसचाणूरमर्दनम्
देवकीपरमानन्दं कृष्णं वंदे जगद्गुरुम् ॥ १ ॥

vasudeva-sutam devam kansa-chāṇūra-mardanam
devakī-paramānandam kṛiṣhṇam vande jagadgurum

We bow down to Lord Krishna, the son of Vasudev. He defeated the demons Kansa and Chanur, among his many feats. He brings joy to his mother, Devaki, and is the Supreme Master of the world.

Krishna Stotram

मूकं करोति वाचालं पंगुं लंघयते गिरिम् ।
यत्कृपा तमहं वन्दे परमानंदं माधवम् ॥

mūkam karoti vāchālam paṅgum laṅghayate girim
yatkṛipā tamaham vande paramānanda-mādhavam

We show great respect to Lord Krishna, who is like a giant ocean of happiness! He's so amazing that with his grace and special help even one who can't talk can suddenly say super smart things and one who can't walk can climb a huge mountain.

Ram Stotram

शुद्धब्रह्मपरात्पर राम् ।
कालात्मकपरमेश्वर राम् ॥
शेषतल्पसुखनिद्रित राम् ।
शेषतल्पसुखनिद्रित राम् ॥
ब्रह्माद्यामरप्रार्थित राम् ।
राम् राम् जय राजा राम् ॥
राम् राम् जय सीता राम् ॥

śuddhabrahmaparātpara rām
kālātmakaparameśvara rām
śeṣatalpasukhanidrita rām
śeṣatalpasukhanidrita rām
brahmādyāmaraprārthita rām
rām rām jaya rājā rām
rām rām jaya sītā rām

When things get tough, I find safety in Lord Ram. He's the ultimate good guy, the strongest of the strong, like the master of time, who always knows what's happening. He's so powerful, he can even relax on a giant snake bed. Even the strongest of gods, like the strong Brahma, asked Lord Ram for His help. He's almost like a superhero for the gods, ready to tackle any trouble!

Ram Stuti

श्री रामचन्द्र कृपालु भजुमन
हरण भवभय दारुणं ।
नव कंज लोचन कंज मुख
कर कंज पद कंजारुणं ॥१॥

śrī rāmacandra kṛpālu bhajumana
haraṇa bhavabhaya dāruṇam |
nava kaṃja locana kaṃja mukha
kara kaṃja pada kaṃjāruṇam ||

Sing along praises about Lord Ram, the super brave hero who protects us from all scary things, including death! He's so amazing, his eyes, mouth, hands and feet all look as beautiful as brand new, bright red flowers! .

... this stuti is continued to the next page

Ram Stuti

कन्दर्प अगणित अमित छवि
नव नील नीरद सुन्दरं ।
पटपीत मानहुँ तडित रुचि शुचि
नोमि जनक सुतावरं ॥२॥

kandarpa agaṇita amita chavi
nava nīla nīrada sundaraṃ |
paṭapīta mānahuṁ taḍita ruci śuci
nomi janaka sutāvaraṃ ||2||

Lord Ram is more handsome than a whole bunch of superheroes! His skin is as smooth and blue as a fresh summer cloud, and his clothes are bright yellow like lightning flashing across the sky. He's married to Sita, who's the daughter of a king named Janak.

... this stuti is continued to the next page

Ram Stuti

भजु दीनबन्धु दिनेश दानव
दैत्य वंश निकन्दनं ।
रघुनन्द आनन्द कन्द कोशल
चन्द दशरथ नन्दनं ॥३॥

bhaju dīnabandhu dineśa dānava
daitya vaṃśa nikandanam |
raghunanda ānanda kanda kośala
chand daśaratha nandanam ||3||

Sing along praises of Lord Rama, the best friend anyone could ask for, especially those in need! He's so powerful that he is also known as the lord of the sun! He chased away all the demons and cleansed the world of demons from the lineage of Danu and Ditiy. He brought happiness to his mother's Kosala dynasty, just like fluffy clouds and a bright moon bring sunshine after a storm. He's also super loved by his family, especially his dad, King Dashrath.

... this stuti is continued to the next page

Ram Stuti

शिर मुकुट कुंडल तिलक
चारु उदारु अङ्ग विभूषणं ।
आजानु भुज शर चाप धर
संग्राम जित खरदूषणं ॥४॥

śira mukuṭa kuṃḍala tilaka
cāru udāru aṅga vibhūṣaṇaṃ |
ājānu bhuja śara cāpa dhara
saṃgrāma jita kharadūṣaṇaṃ ||4||

Let's sing praises to Sri Ram! He wears a beautiful crown on His head, shiny earrings and has a special mark (tilak) on His forehead. His body is decorated with lovely ornaments. His long arms reach down to His knees, and He holds a bow and arrow. He is the hero who won the battle against Khar and Dushan.

... this stuti is continued to the next page

Ram Stuti

iti vadati tulasīdāsa śaṃkara
śeṣa muni mana raṃjanaṃ |
mam hṛdaya kaṃja nivāsa kuru
kāmādi khaladala gaṃjanaṃ ||5||

Tulsidas prays that Lord Ram, who makes Lord Shiva, Sheshnag and the other saints happy, always lives in his heart and helps him get rid of bad feelings like anger, greed and desire.

... this stuti is continued to the next page

Ram Stuti

मन जाहि राच्यो मिलहि सो
वर सहज सुन्दर सांवरो ।
करुणा निधान सुजान शील
स्नेह जानत रावरो ॥६॥

mana jāhi rācyo milahi so
vara sahaja sundara sāṃvaro |
karuṇā nidhāna sujāna śīla
sneha jānata rāvaro ||6||

Whatever you love in your mind, you can find that same goodness in Lord Ram. He is very kind and wise.

... this stuti is continued to the next page

Ram Stuti

When everyone heard Mother Parvati's (Gauri) blessings, they all, including Janaki (Sita), felt happy. Tulsidas says that after praying to Bhavani many times, Sitaji happily went back to the palace.

Goddess Saraswati

या कुन्देन्दुतुषारहारधवला या शुभ्रवस्त्रावृता
या वीणावरदण्डमण्डितकरा या श्वेतपद्मासना ।
या ब्रह्माच्युतशंकरप्रभृतिभिर्देवः सदा पूजिता
सा मां पातु सरस्वति भगवती निःशेषजाड्यापहा ॥१॥

yā kundendu-tuṣāra-hāradhavalā yā śubhra-vastrāvṛtā
yā vīṇā-varadaṇ-ḍamaṇḍitakarā yā śveta-padmāsanā |
yā brahmā-cyutaśaṃ-karaprabhṛti-bhirdevaḥ sadā pūjitā
sā māṃ pātu sarasvati bhagavatī niḥśeṣajāḍyāpahā ||

I bow to Goddess Saraswati. She is as white as jasmine flowers, as cool as the moon, as bright as snow and shines like a string of pearls. She wears pure white clothes. She holds a musical instrument called veena and a staff that grants wishes. She sits on a pure white lotus flower and is a favourite of Lord Brahma, Lord Vishnu, Lord Shiva and other gods. O Goddess Saraswati, please protect me and help me understand everything.

Dhanvantri Strotram

ॐ नमो भागवते वासुदेवाय धन्वन्तरये अमृतकलश हस्ताय
सर्वा-मय विनाशनाय त्रैलोक्यनाथय श्री महाविष्णवे नमः

oṁ namo bhagavate mahāsudarśhanāya vāsudevāya
dhanvantarāyeḥ
amṛitakalaśha hastāya sarva bhayavināśhāya sarva
roganivāraṇāya
trilokapathāya trilokanāthāya śhrī
mahāviṣhṇusvarūpa
śhrīdhanvantarī svarūpa śhrī śhrī śhrī auṣhadhachakra
nārāyaṇāya namaḥ

We pay our respects to Lord Dhanvantari, who is also called Vasudev and Maha-Sudarshan. He carries a pot of special healing potion and takes away people's fears. He cures all sickness and helps those who are ill. He travels everywhere and rules over everything. We salute Lord Dhanvantari, who is a form of Maha-Vishnu and is worshipped as the Lord of medicines. He knows all about medicines and how they work.

Shlokas
from
The Gita

Karmanye Vadhika Raste

कर्मण्येवाधिकारस्ते
मा फलेषु कदाचन ।
मा कर्मफलहेतुर्भूर्मा
ते सङ्गोऽस्त्वकर्मणि ॥

karmaṇye-vādhikā-raste
mā phaleṣu kadācana |
mā karma-phala-heturbhūrmā
te saṅgo'stva-karmaṇi||

Do your best, but don't worry about getting a prize.
When you have a job to do, just focus on doing it well.
Don't only do things because you want a reward, and
don't get sad if you don't get one.

Yada Yada Hi Dharmasya

यदा यदा हि धर्मस्य
ग्लानिर्भवति भारत ।
अभ्युत्थानमधर्मस्य
तदात्मानं सृजाम्यहम् ॥

yadā yadā hi dharmasya
glānirbhavati bhārata |
abhyutthānam-adharmasya
tadātmānaṃ sṛjāmyaham ||

Good always wins in the end. Sometimes, people might not be very nice. But at the end good things are more powerful and will eventually win. So, be a good person yourself and help make the world a better place!

Yogasthah Kuru Karmani

योगस्थः कुरु कर्माणि
सङ्गं त्यक्त्वा धनञ्जय।
सिद्ध्यसिद्ध्योः समो भूत्वा
समत्वं योग उच्यते।।

yogasthaḥ kuru karmāṇi
saṅgaṃ tyaktvā dhanañjaya |
siddhyasiddhyoḥ samo bhūtvā
samatvaṃ yoga ucyate||

Stay calm and focus while you learn. This verse is like a tip for studying. It says to be calm and relaxed, just like the famous warrior Arjuna. Don't worry too much about getting the best grades, just focus on learning as much as you can. Being calm and focused while you learn is like a superpower that helps you grow!

Nasato Vidyate Bhavo

नासतो विद्यते भावो नाभावो विद्यते सतः।
उभयोरपि दृष्टोऽन्तस्त्वनयोस्तत्त्वदर्शिभिः॥

nāsato vidyate bhāvo nābhāvo vidyate sataḥ |
ubhayorapi dṛṣṭo'ntastvanayostattvadarśibhiḥ ||

This verse talks about what's real and what's not. Imagine things you can touch and see, like toys or animals—those are real. Now imagine things you only dream about, like flying dragons—those aren't real. Smart people who study a lot have figured this out, and this verse says they know the difference between real and make-believe!

Uddhared Atman Atmanam

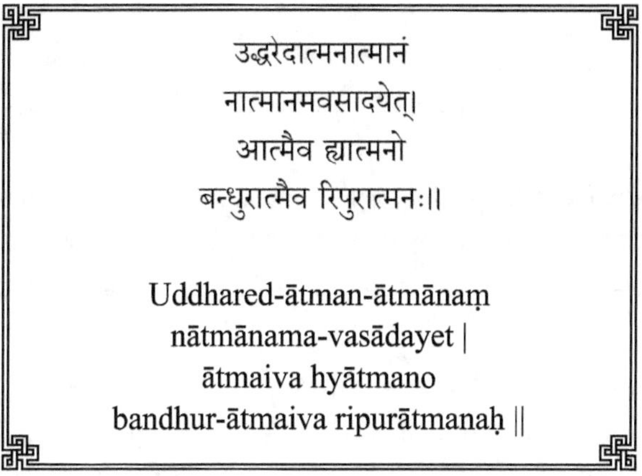

Believe in yourself and keep trying! You have the power to make yourself better, just like a superhero. You can be your own best friend by setting goals and working hard to achieve them. Don't give up on yourself—be your own cheerleader and keep learning and growing!

Tasmadyuddhaya Yujyasva

तस्माद्युद्धाय युज्यस्व योगी संख्येऽपि योग्यताम्।
एकं वाक्षरमच्युतं यज्ञ इच्छामि तद् ब्रह्म।।

tasmādyuddhāya yujyasva yogī saṃkhye'pi yogyatām |
ekaṃ vākṣaramacyutaṃ yajña icchāmi tad brahma ||

This verse is like a reminder to keep your eyes on the prize, just like when you're playing a game and want to win. Imagine you have a big project or test coming up. To do your best, you need to focus and avoid distractions. It's like putting on blinders like a racehorse so you can concentrate on learning as much as possible. The more you focus on your studies, the closer you get to reaching your goals and becoming a super-learner!

Na Hi Jnanena Sadarsham

न हि ज्ञानेन सदृशं
पवित्रमिह विद्यते।
तत्स्वयं योगसंसिद्धः
कालेनात्मनि विन्दति॥

na hi jñānena sadṛśaṃ
pavitramiha vidyate |
tatsvayaṃ yogasaṃsiddhaḥ
kālenātmani vindati ||

This verse says learning new things is a booster shot for your brain! The more you learn, the cleaner and sharper your mind gets. And guess what? The more you learn and practice, the better you get at learning even more—it's like a superpower that keeps growing!

Tasmad Asaktah Statam

तस्मादसक्तः सततं कार्यं कर्म समाचर ।
असक्तो ह्याचरन् कर्म परं आप्नोति पूरुषः॥

tasmād asaktaḥ satataṁ kāryaṁ karma samāchara |
asakto hyācharan karma param āpnoti pūruṣaḥ ||

This verse talks about doing things because they're the right thing to do, not to get a reward. Imagine you have a chore, like cleaning your room. It's best to do your chore because it needs to be done, not because you want a prize. When you do things the right way, without expecting something in return, it makes you a good person!

Sukha-dukhe Same Kritva

सुखदुःखे समे कृत्वा लाभालाभौ जयाजयौ।
ततो युद्धाय युज्यस्व नैवं पापमवाप्स्यसि॥

sukha-duḥkhe same kṛitvā lābhālābhau jayājayau |
tato yuddhāya yujyasva naivaṁ pāpam avāpsyasi ||

This verse is like advice from a wise teacher before a big exam. It says to focus on studying itself, not on getting very high or very low marks, or on feeling happy or sad. If you just play your best and do what you're supposed to do, you won't get in trouble. Imagine you're in a friendly competition with your friends. You should focus on playing fair and having fun, not on winning at all costs. That way, everyone enjoys the game!

Shraddhavan Labhate Jñānam

श्रद्धावाँल्लभते ज्ञानं तत्परः संयतेन्द्रियः ।
ज्ञानं लब्ध्वा परां शान्तिमचिरेणाधिगच्छति ॥

śhraddhāvān labhate jñānaṁ tat-paraḥ sanyatendriyaḥ |
jñānaṁ labdhvā parāṁ śhāntim achireṇādhigachchhati ||

This verse is like a secret to unlocking super powers! It says that if you believe really strongly and try your hardest, you can learn to control your mind and feelings. When you can do that, you can then unlock special knowledge, like a hidden treasure! This knowledge is like a magic key that helps you find lasting peace and happiness, like finding a hidden paradise!

Prayers

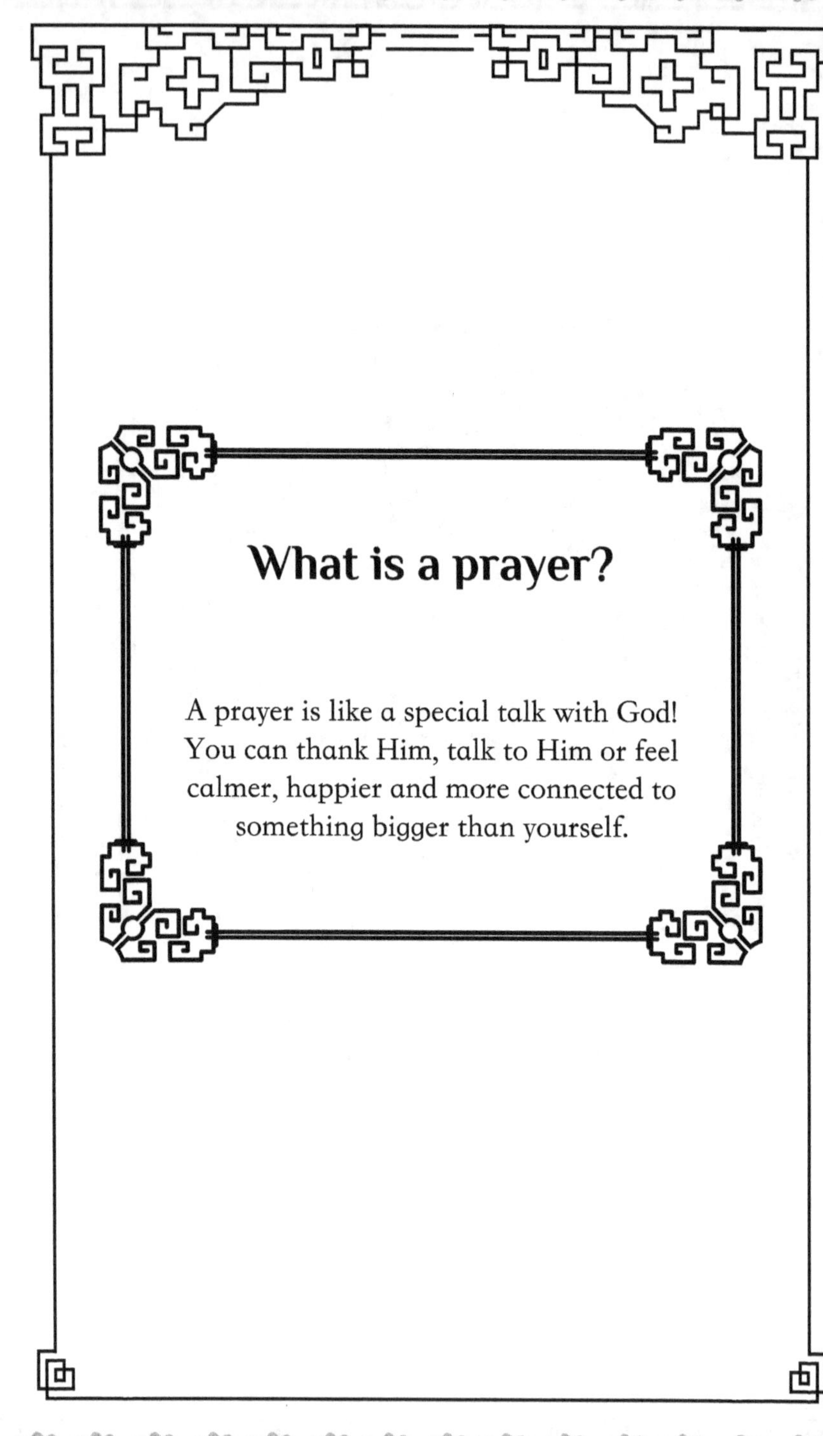

What is a prayer?

A prayer is like a special talk with God! You can thank Him, talk to Him or feel calmer, happier and more connected to something bigger than yourself.

Morning Prayer

Lord, help me to live this day, quietly, easily;
to lean on your great strength, trustfully, restfully;
to wait for the unfolding of your will, patiently, serenely;
to meet others, peacefully, joyfully;
to face tomorrow, confidently, courageously.
- St Francis of Assis

For Being Grateful

Shout for joy to the Lord, all the earth.
Worship the Lord with gladness;
come before him with joyful songs.
Know that the Lord is God.
It is He who made us, and we are his;
we are his people, the sheep of his pasture.
Enter his gates with thanksgiving and his courts with praise;
Give thanks to him and praise his name.
For the Lord is good and his love endures forever;
His faithfulness continues through all generations.
Psalm 100

For Peace

Make me a channel of your peace.
Where there is hatred let me bring your love.
Where there is injury, your pardon, Lord
And where there's doubt, true faith in you.
Make me a channel of your peace
Where there's despair in life, let me bring hope
Where there is darkness, only light
And where there's sadness, ever joy.
Oh, Master grant that I may never seek
So much to be consoled as to console
To be understood as to understand
To be loved as to love with all my soul.
Make me a channel of your peace
It is in pardoning that we are pardoned
In giving to all men that we receive
And in dying that we're born to eternal life.

For Forgiveness and Redemption

Amazing grace! how sweet the sound,
That saved a wretch; like me!
I once was lost, but now am found,
Was blind, but now I see.
'Twas grace that taught my heart to fear,
And grace my fears relieved;
How precious did that grace appear
The hour I first believed!
The Lord hath promised good to me,
His word my hope secures;
He will my shield and portion be
As long as life endures.
When we've been there ten thousand years,
Bright shining as the sun,
We've no less days to sing God's praise
Than when we first begun.

- John Newton

In Praise of the Lord

Our Father, who art in heaven,
hallowed be thy name;
thy kingdom come;
thy will be done;
on earth as it is in heaven.
Give us this day our daily bread.
And forgive us our trespasses,
as we forgive those who trespass against us.
And lead us not into temptation;
but deliver us from evil.
For thine is the kingdom,
the power, and the glory,
for ever and ever.
Amen.

For Strength

The Lord is my rock,
and my fortress, and my deliverer;
My God, my strength,
In whom I will trust.
- Psalm 18:2
The Lord is my strength and my shield,
My heart trusts in him, and he helps me.
My heart leaps for joy,
And with my song I praise him.
Psalm 28:7

With Gratitude

All things bright and beautiful,
All creatures great and small,
All things wise and wonderful,
The Lord God made them all.
Each little flower that opens,
Each little bird that sings,
He made their glowing colours,
He made their tiny wings.
The purple-headed mountain,
The river running by,
The sunset and the morning
That brightens up the sky.
The cold wind in the winter,
The pleasant summer sun,
The ripe fruits in the garden,
He made them, every one.
He gave us eyes to see them,
And lips that we might tell
How great is God Almighty,
Who has made all things well.

Before Meals

The Lord's Prayer
Our Father, who art in heaven,
hallowed be thy name;
thy kingdom come;
thy will be done;
on earth as it is in heaven.
Give us this day our daily bread.
And forgive us our trespasses,
as we forgive those who trespass against us.
And lead us not into temptation;
but deliver us from the evil one.
For thine is the kingdom,
the power, and the glory,
for ever and ever. Amen.

For Guidance

Heavenly Father, lead me in Your ways
And guide my steps according to Your will.
Illuminate the path before me
And grant me wisdom to make righteous decisions.
Help me to follow
Your guidance faithfully.
For Comfort
Loving God, in times of sorrow and grief,
Wrap Your comforting arms around me.
Console me with Your love, and
Bring healing to my broken heart.
Grant me the assurance of Your presence, and
The hope of eternal life with You.

www.ingramcontent.com/pod-product-compliance
Lightning Source LLC
LaVergne TN
LVHW011024200726
843509LV00011B/1190